D1586889

HighTide, Theatr Clwyd and Vicky Graham Productions in
association with The Yard Theatre present

PILGRIMS

A world premiere by Elinor Cook

Pilgrims premiered at HighTide Festival 2016 on 8 September 2016.
Pilgrims then transferred to The Yard Theatre with Vicky Graham Productions
from 20 September–15 October before transferring to Theatr Clwyd from
18–29 October 2016 in a production directed by Tamara Harvey, Artistic
Director of Theatr Clwyd.

Supported by
The Peter Wolff Trust

Supported using public funding by
**ARTS COUNCIL
ENGLAND**

PILGRIMS

Presented by HighTide, Theatr Clywd and Vicky Graham
Productions in association with The Yard Theatre

RACHEL	Amanda Wilkin
WILL	Steffan Donnelly
DAN	Jack Monaghan
DIRECTOR	Tamara Harvey
DESIGN	James Perkins
LIGHTING	Nic Holdridge
SOUND AND COMPOSITION	Jared Zeus
ASSOCIATE DESIGNER	Victoria Smart
PRODUCTION MANAGER	Tom Nickson
STAGE MANAGER	Paul Sawtell

CAST

AMANDA WILKIN | RACHEL
Amanda performed in *Hamlet* with Shakespeare's Globe, which toured to every nation over two years.

Theatre includes *Hamlet, Gabriel, The Tempest* (Shakespeare's Globe); *Hopelessly Devoted* (Paines Plough/Birmingham Repertory); *Arabian Nights* (Watermill); *The Bacchae, Blood Wedding* (Royal & Derngate); *Marat/Sade; A Midsummer Night's Dream* (RSC); *Stamping, Shouting and Singing Home* (Nuffield); *The Twits* (Dukes).

Television includes *Doctors* (BBC1); *Gavin and Stacey* (BBC3. Baby Cow Productions)

STEFFAN DONNELLY | WILL
Steffan trained at Guildhall School of Music and Drama.

Theatre includes: *The Winter's Tale, Pericles, Romeo and Juliet, A Midsummer Night's Dream, Titus Andronicus* (Shakespeare's Globe); *Y Twr/The Tower* (Invertigo tour); *A World Elsewhere* (Theatre503); *Journeying Boys* (Barbican); *Outside on the Street* (Pleasance Edinburgh/Arcola); *The Winslow Boy* (Theatr Clwyd); *Saer Doliau/Doll Mender* (Finborough); *I am Not Manuel* (Teatre Lliure, Barcelona).

Television includes: *London Spy* (BBC).

Steffan is Joint Artistic Director of Invertigo Theatre Company, and has adapted *My People* (co-production with Theatr Clwyd), and is currently developing their new one-man show, *My Body Welsh*.

JACK MONAGHAN | DAN
Jack Monaghan studied Natural Sciences at Cambridge University.

Theatre includes: *As You Like It* (Shakespeare's Globe); *Deposit* (Hampstead); *Regeneration* (Royal & Derngate/UK tour); *Wendy and Peter Pan* (RSC); *The Shawshank Redemption* (Assembly Rooms); *Cinderella and the Midnight Princess* (Rose, Kingston); *The Merchant of Venice* (Saïd Amphitheatre, Oxford); *War Horse* (West End); *Love on the Dole* (Finborough); *The Fading Hum* (Manchester Theatre Festival).

Television includes: *Jack Taylor* (ZDF, Telegael); *The Ark* (BBC); *Black Mirror* (Zeppotron, Channel 4).

Film includes: *Love's Lost* (Fizz and Ginger Films); *The Somnambulists* (Alan Mckenna Films).

CREATIVES

ELINOR COOK | WRITER

Elinor was the winner of the George Devine Award for Most Promising Playwright 2013. She is currently under commission to Paines Plough, the Gate Theatre and Warwick Arts Centre, and is writing an adaptation of Mac Barnett's *Extra Yarn* for The Orange Tree Theatre.

Elinor's plays include: *The Rehearsal* (LAMDA); *Ten Weeks* (Paines Plough/Royal Welsh College of Music and Drama); *Image of an Unknown Young Woman* (The Gate); *The Boy Preference* (National Theatre Connections); *The Girl's Guide to Saving The World* (HighTide Festival); *this is where we got to when you came in* (Bush/non zero one).

Elinor also wrote an episode of *The Secrets* for BBC One, directed by Dominic Savage.

TAMARA HARVEY | DIRECTOR

Tamara is the Artistic Director of Theatr Clwyd. She has directed in the West End, throughout the UK and abroad, working on classic plays, new writing, musical theatre and in film. Her inaugural production for Theatr Clwyd was *Much Ado About Nothing* in May 2016.

Premiere theatre includes: *From Here to Eternity* (Shaftesbury); *Breeders* (St James); *The Kitchen Sink*, *The Contingency Plan*, *Sixty-Six Books*, tHe d'YsFUnCKshOnalZ! (Bush); *Elephants*, *In the Vale of Health*, *Hello/Goodbye*, *Blue Heart Afternoon* (Hampstead); *Plague Over England* (Finborough/West End).

Other West End includes: *Bash* (Trafalgar Studios); *Whipping It Up* (New Ambassadors); *One Flew Over the Cuckoo's Nest* (Gielgud/Garrick).

Other theatre includes: *Kreutzer vs Kreutzer* (Sam Wanamaker Playhouse); *Pride and Prejudice* (Sheffield Crucible); *Educating Rita*, *Smash* (Menier Chocolate Factory/Theatre Royal Bath); *Romeo and Juliet* (Theatre of Memory at Middle Temple Hall); *Much Ado About Nothing* (Shakespeare's Globe); *Dancing at Lughnasa* (Birmingham Rep); *Bedroom Farce* (West Yorkshire Playhouse); *The Importance of Being Earnest* (Shakespeare Theatre of New Jersey); *Closer* (Theatre Royal Northampton); *Tell Me On a Sunday* (UK tour) *Something Cloudy, Something Clear* (Finborough).

Tamara directed the Shakespeare scenes that form an integral part of *Anonymous*, the feature film by Roland Emmerich. She was Associate Artistic Director of the Bush Theatre in 2010–11, overseeing the move to the Bush's new home and directing the first three productions in the new theatre. Tamara is a Trustee of the Peggy Ramsay Foundation and of the National Student Drama Festival and has twice been a panel member for the George Devine Award for Most Promising Playwright. She is a graduate of the University of Bristol and trained at the Shakespeare Theatre of New Jersey.

JAMES PERKINS | DESIGNER

James is an associate of Forward Theatre Project and one third of papers/scissors/stone, and created *Story Whores*.

Theatre includes: *Jess and Joe*, *German Skerries* (Orange Tree); *Last Five Years* (New Wolsey); *Little Shop of Horrors* (Royal Exchange); *Breeders* (St James); *Shiver*, *Lost in Yonkers* (Watford Palace Theatre); *Ciphers* (Bush/Out of Joint); *1001 Nights* (Unicorn/ Transport); *Liar Liar* (Unicorn); *Girl in the Yellow Dress* (Salisbury Playhouse); *Microcosm* (Soho); *Dances of Death* (Gate); *The Fantasist's Waltz* (York Theatre Royal); *Stockwell* (Tricycle); *Carthage*; *Foxfinder*, *The Bofors Gun*, *Trying* (Finborough); *Lizzie Finn*, *Floyd Collins* (Southwark Playhouse); *The Marriage of Figaro* (Wilton's Music Hall, Musqiue Cordiale); *The Life of Stuff*,

Desolate Heaven, Threads, Many Moons (Theatre503); *The Hotel Plays* (Grange Hotel); *St John's Night, Matters of Life and Death* (Contemporary Dane UK tour); *Iolanthe, The Way Through the Woods* (Pleasance); *The Faerie Queen* (Sadler's Wells); *The Wonder* (Battersea Arts Centre);

NICHOLAS HOLDRIDGE | LIGHTING

Theatre includes: *The Hotels Plays* (The Grange Hotel Holbon); *The Firebird* (English National Ballet, London Coliseum); *Scott Mills The Musical* (Pleasance); *Xerxes* (Iford Arts); *Uncle Vanya* (Wilton's Music Hall); *The Promise* (Mercury); *The Immodest Tease Show* (KOKO Camden); *The Yeomen of the Guard* (Opera Della Luna, Buxton Opera House); *Deathwatch, House of Bones, The Criminals, Till Death Do Us Part* (Drama Centre London, The Platform Theatre); *The Go!Go!Go! Show* (Empire Leicester Square); *The Mikado, Beowulf the Pantomime, La bohème, The Pirates of Penzance; The Three Musketeers* (Charles Court Opera/The King's Head/tour); *A Single Act, Yellow Card* (Step Out Arts, Pavillion Dance).

JARED ZEUS | SOUND AND COMPOSITION

Jared is a graduate of Ithaca College USA and trained at the Shakespeare Theatre of New Jersey. Jared was the main songwriter for *Former Future* and is also the writer and composer of the new pop musical *Stay.*

Theatre includes: *Cat On a Hot Tin Roof* (Theatr Clwyd); *Hello Goodbye, In the Vale of Health* (Hampstead); *Breeders* (St James); *Where the Mangrove Grows* (Theatre503); *Tartuffe* (Shakespeare Theatre of New Jersey); *Twelfth Night; Love's Labour's Lost; A Midsummer Night's Dream* (Lamb Players).

Television includes: *Where Are We; Someday; Worth the Wait* (None in the Oven); *Take Me Home; Worth the Wait* (Medium); *The Scenic Route; Fat Hammond's Banjo Lounge* (pilot).

VICTORIA SMART | ASSOCIATE DESIGNER

Victoria Smart trained in Design for Performance at Wimbledon College of Art. She also works as a prop and model maker and collaborates on artist-led projects.

Theatre includes: *Carnival Journeys* (V&A/Complicite) *Enduring Song* (Southwark Playhouse); *The Last March* (Bikeshed, Southwark Playhouse); *Maria 1968* (Edinburgh Fringe); *Billy Chickens is a Psychopath Superstar* (Theatre503/Latitude).

As costume assistant and supervisor: *German Skerries* (Orange Tree); *Sisters* (East15 Acting School); *P'yongyang* (Finborough); *Oliver!* (Curve); *Life of Stuff* (Theatre503).

Film includes: *Nether.*

TOM NICKSON | PRODUCTION MANAGER

Tom was Head of Production at Hampstead Theatre for seven years.

For Hampstead Theatre: *Chariots of Fire, Race, Hysteria, Sunny Afternoon, Hello Goodbye, Stevie, Matchbox, Rabbithole, Reasons to be Happy, The Mystae, Ken, Pine, Blue Heart Afternoon.*

Other theatre includes: *Impossible* (Noël Coward); *Sunny Afternoon* (Harold Pinter); *Idomeneo, L'italiana in Algeri* (Garsington); *TATINOF* (UK and international tour); *Sideways* (St James)

H|GH
T|DE

A MAJOR PLATFORM FOR NEW PLAYWRIGHTS

HighTide is a theatre company.

We produce new plays in an annual festival in Aldeburgh, Suffolk and on tour.

Our programming influences the mainstream. Our work takes place in the here and now.

HighTide: Adventurous theatre for adventurous people.

LANSONS
Advice Ideas Results

Esmée
Fairbairn
FOUNDATION

BackstageTrust

Supported using public funding by
ARTS COUNCIL
ENGLAND

united agents
THE LITERARY & TALENT AGENCY

HIGH TIDE

2016

A DECADE OF INFLUENCING THE MAINSTREAM

Our tenth anniversary season commenced with the world premiere of Anders Lustgarten's **The Sugar-Coated Bullets of the Bourgeoisie** at Arcola Theatre ahead of opening HighTide Festival 2016.

Rob Drummond's **In Fidelity** premiered at the Traverse Theatre before opening HighTide Festival 2016.

HighTide Festival 2016 premiered new works by Theresa Ikoko, Elinor Cook, Anders Lustgarten and Rob Drummond as well as a special HighTide Anniversary production of **The Path**, featuring writing by Luke Barnes, EV Crowe, Vickie Donoghue, Thomas Eccleshare, Ella Hickson, Harry Melling and Vinay Patel.

Theresa Ikoko's debut production **Girls** transferred to Birmingham Repertory Theatre and Soho Theatre following its premiere at HighTide Festival 2016.

Elinor Cook's **Pilgrims** transferred to the Yard Theatre and Theatr Clwyd following its premiere at HighTide Festival 2016.

Al Smith's seminal play **Harrogate** will receive its London premiere at the Royal Court Theatre ahead of a national tour with house in Autumn 2016.

Our final 10th anniversary production, **The Brolly Project**, will premiere at the Young Vic Theatre in February 2017 with Look Left Look Right and the Young Vic Theatre.

For full details, visit hightide.org.uk

HIGH TIDE

24a St John Street, London, EC1M 4AY
0207 566 9765 - hello@hightide.org.uk - hightide.org.uk

HighTide Company

Artistic Director Steven Atkinson
General Manager Robyn Keynes
Administrative Assistant Holly White
Creative Associate Andrew Twyman
HighTide Mascot Charlie the Dog

Executive Producer Francesca Clark
Marketing Officer Freddie Porter
New Work Manager Marcelo Dos Santos
Resident Writer Melanie Spencer

First Commissions: Writers on Attachment
Nina Segal; Christopher York; Healah Riazi; Jon Barton; Sophie Ellerby.

In 2016 - 17 HighTide has collaborated with
Arcola Theatre; Arts Educational; Birmingham Repertory Theatre; Chichester Festival Theatre; house; Look Left Look Right; Royal Court Theatre; Soho Theatre; Talawa Theatre Company; Theatr Clwyd; Traverse Theatre; Vicky Graham Productions; Yard Theatre; Young Vic Theatre.

Board
Steven Atkinson; Nancy Durrant; Sue Emmas; Nick Giles; Diana Hiddleston; Priscilla John; Mark Lacey; Criona Palmer (Chair); Clare Parsons; Vinay Patel; Graham White.

Advisory Council
Jack Bradley; Robert Fox; Thelma Holt CBE; Joyce Hytner OBE; Mel Kenyon; Tom Morris; Dallas Smith; Roger Wingate.

Patrons
Sinead Cusack; Stephen Daldry CBE; Sir Richard Eyre CBE; Sally Greene OBE; Sir David Hare; Sir Nicholas Hytner; Sam Mendes CBE; Juliet Stevenson CBE.

H|GH T|DE

WE NEED YOUR SUPPORT

There are very talented young playwrights in the UK, and if they are lucky they will find their way to the HighTide FestivalTheatre season in Suffolk. I hope you will join me in supporting this remarkable and modest organisation. With your help HighTide can play an even more major role in the promoting of new writing in the UK.

— Lady Susie Sainsbury, Backstage Trust

HighTide is a registered charity and we could not champion the next generation of theatre artists and create world-class productions for you without ticket sales, fundraising, sponsorship and public investment.

To undertake our work this year we need to raise over £750,000.

We need your help to make these targets. You can show your support by: making a donation; buying Festival tickets; recommending the Festival to your friends; donating your time to help work on the Festival; writing to your local councillor and MPs about how much you value the HighTide Festival.

If you would like to discuss making a donation to HighTide, please speak to freddie@hightide.org.uk or call on 0207 566 9765.

We are thankful to all of our supporters, without whom our work simply would not take place.

Leading Partner: Lansons

Trusts and Foundations
Boris Karloff Charitable Foundation; Cockayne Grants for the Arts; Esmeé Fairbairn Foundation; Harold Hyam Wingate Foundation; London Community Foundation; Mackintosh Foundation; Martin Bowley Charitable Trust; The Old Possum's Practical TrustParham Trust; Peter Wolff Trust.

Major Funder: Backstage Trust

Individual Supporters
Sam Fogg; Clare Parsons and Tony Langham; Tony Mackintosh and Criona Palmer; Lady Susie Sainsbury; Albert and Marjorie Scardino.

Corporate Sponsors
John Clayton and Bishops Printers; United Agents.

H|GH
T|DE

LANSONS CONGRATULATES
HIGHTIDE ON THEIR
10TH ANNIVERSARY

Since 2008, HighTide and Lansons have celebrated a year-on-year partnership that is unique. Lansons is a highly regarded reputation management and PR firm whose work is largely split between building reputations for organisations growing rapidly in the market and protecting reputations of those facing challenges. This partnership was awarded three silver Corporate Engagement Awards in 2016, and has been featured in the Evening Standard and The Guardian as an example of innovative collaboration between a business and an arts charity.

Lansons donates office space, meeting rooms, reception services and IT support year-round to HighTide, which allows them to fully re-invest all of their earned income and charitable support straight into their work. HighTide offers Lansons the opportunity to engage with the culture sector by attending their productions.

Both HighTide and Lansons are proud of this mutually beneficial relationship, and hope that by being transparent about the nature of it, more businesses and charities will endeavour to explore working together.

LANSONS
Advice Ideas Results

Theatr Clwyd

'One of the hidden treasures of North Wales, a huge vibrant culture complex'

Guardian

Theatr Clwyd produces exciting, dynamic, vibrant theatre for Wales and beyond. Led by Artistic Director Tamara Harvey we are a champion of world-class drama, new writing and family-friendly work. Overlooking the Clwydian Hills yet only forty minutes from Liverpool we have three theatres, a cinema, café, bar and three art galleries to offer a rich and varied programme of visual arts, film, theatre, music and comedy. We work extensively with our local community, schools and colleges as well as creating award-winning work for and with young people.

Over 200,000 people a year come through our doors and in 2015 Theatr Clwyd was voted the Most Welcoming Theatre in Wales.

'Absolute must-see productions' *Western Mail*

01352 701521
www.theatrclwyd.com

VICKY GRAHAM
VGP P R O D U C T I O N S

Established in May 2012 with the support of the Stage One Bursary Scheme, Vicky Graham Productions develops and produces brave, quality new theatre in collaboration with the most inventive, forward-thinking artists and partners. Its independent, ambitious approach to producing aims to achieve the greatest possible impact and production life for its artists, shows and supporters. It actively promotes education, learning and skill-sharing within a supportive theatre community to ensure the future strength of the industry.

Since 2012, Vicky Graham Productions has produced the world premieres of *The Sluts of Sutton Drive* by Joshua Conkel (Finborough Theatre), and *Strong Arm* by Finlay Robertson (Winner – Old Vic New Voices Edinburgh Award), as well as three productions by multi award-winning cabaret duo House of Blakewell.

Vicky Graham Productions' commissions include *Breeders* by Ben Ockrent, which was selected to open the inaugural Stage One ONE STAGE Season at the St. James Theatre in September 2014, directed by Tamara Harvey, and *Flowers for Mrs Harris* – a musical adaptation of Paul Gallico's much-loved novel by Rachel Wagstaff and Richard Taylor – which received its first production at Sheffield Theatres in May 2016, directed by Daniel Evans.

★★★★★
'five star fairytale… one of the most heart-warming and tear-forming British musicals of recent years' *Guardian* on *Flowers for Mrs Harris*

www.vickygrahamproductions.com

@VGPtheatre
facebook.com/vickygrahamproductions

Supported using public funding by
**ARTS COUNCIL
ENGLAND**

Vicky Graham Productions receives no regular funding. To find out more about our plans to develop and produce more ambitious theatre, please contact **vicky@vickygrahamproductions.com**

Built in 2011 by Founder and Artistic Director Jay Miller, The Yard is a multi-award winning theatre in Hackney Wick overlooking the Queen Elizabeth Olympic Park. The Yard provides a safe space for artists to grow new ideas, and for audiences to access outstanding new work.

In five years, The Yard has become 'the most important theatre in east London' (*Time Out*). Success includes two transfers to the National Theatre for *Beyond Caring* ('quietly devastating' ★★★★★ *Guardian*) and *Chewing Gum Dreams*, a forthcoming transfer to New York for our sold out production of *The Mikvah Project* ('Every moment feels rich with meaning' ★★★★★ *Time Out*), and numerous awards including two Peter Brook Empty Space awards. Success has also led to partnerships with leading theatres/organisations; current and future project partners include the Young Vic, Royal Court Theatre, National Theatre and HighTide Festival Theatre.

The Yard team is comprised of:

Artistic Director Jay Miller | Executive Director Lucy Oliver-Harrison | Finance & Operations Manager Jack Haynes | Theatre Producer Ashleigh Wheeler | Technical Manager Rhys Denegri | Marketing Manager Rida Hamidou | Music & Events Producer Dan Hampson | Development Officer Gareth Cutter | Local Programmer Katherine Igoe-Ewer | Marketing and Producing Assistant Lara Tysseling | Technical & Buildings Assistant Jessica Barter | Bar Manager Luke McCoy | Bar Duty Managers Tom Hartley & Katie Andrew | Artistic Associates Josh Azouz, Jude Christian, Cheryl Gallagher, Alex Helmsey, Dan Hutton, Simon Holton & Greg Wohead

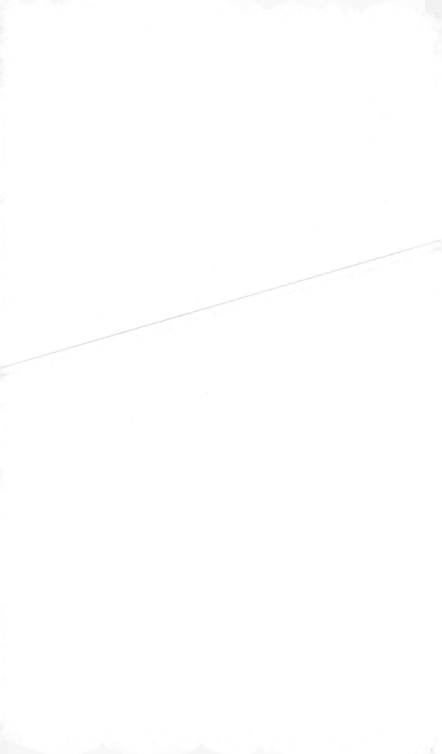

PILGRIMS

Elinor Cook

For Alice

Acknowledgements

My thanks to Phoebe Waller-Bridge, Max Bennet, Tom Mison, Jack Laskey, Geoffrey Streatfield and Rob Mountford who all gave up their time to take part in workshops of early versions of the play; Steven Atkinson and all at HighTide for inviting me back to the festival a second time; Jay Miller at the Yard for his excellent notes; Vicky Graham for her tireless and creative producing; Fay Davies, Emily Hickman and Tumi Belo at the Agency for all their help, kindness and support; and especially to Tamara Harvey who has been instrumental in shaping the play since its earliest inception.

E.C.

'Who gets to speak, and why, is the only question.'

I Love Dick
by Chris Kraus

'The history of the world? Just voices echoing in the dark; images that burn for a few centuries and then fade; stories, old stories, that seem to overlap, strange links, impertinent connections... Our panic and our pain are only eased by a soothing fabulation. We call it history.'

A History of the World in 10 1/2 Chapters
by Julian Barnes

Characters

RACHEL
DAN
WILL

Over the course of the play they shift between their early and late twenties.

A Note on the Text

As far as possible, the play should be performed with very little staging.

All three actors can be on stage at any one time.

They can find a way to use the stage directions as part of the dialogue if that's helpful.

This text went to press before the end of rehearsals and so may differ slightly from the play as performed.

 # 1

A mountain.

The present.

DAN *and* WILL *are sitting side by side.*

DAN *is facing the audience, holding a torch.*

WILL *is facing away.*

RACHEL *is watching them.*

RACHEL   Two men are alone on a mountain.
The men are handsome.
The men are tall.
The men are Caucasian.
Their journey has been long.
Their journey has been linear.
It is a Hero's Tale.
They have been tested.
By beasts.
Storms.
Riddles.
Mirages.
Sirens.
Wicked queens.
All the usual hero things.
The story is nearly over.
The grail is nearly won…

DAN *turns the torch on.*

The beam is very faint.

DAN   Battery's dying.
In the torch.
You got any more, Will?
Will?

Silence.

Tell you what.
I'll go and find someone.
Somewhere.
Someone with batteries.
Won't be long.

Silence.

I'll leave my pack here.
So you'll know.
That I'm coming back.

Silence.

Wouldn't leave you here, Will.
Promise.

Silence.

Hey??
Remember that time in Greenland?
When the ice cracked and I…
I went through?!
The ice!
I went blue all over.
You put your arms around me.
The heat from your body brought mine back to life.
Remember?

Silence.

And our guide!
He only had half a face.
He'd shot the other half clean off!
He wanted to die but he got it wrong.
The angle.
So he had to go through life with this…
Half a face.
Half a nose, shattered cheekbone.
Blind in one eye.
You didn't stare at him.
I did.
I stared at him all the time.
Still dream about him.
Sometimes he's sitting at the end of my bed.

Silence.

He opens his water bottle, drinks from it.

There's nothing in it.

Hey, pass me yours, would you?

Silence.

Will?

RACHEL   Doesn't it hurt?
             Carrying that great big thing.

DAN   What?

RACHEL   Bet it digs into your back.

DAN   Oh.
             Well, it's padded you see.

RACHEL   I see.

DAN   It's an Alpine Classic.

RACHEL   Ah ha.

DAN   Expensive.
             But worth it.

RACHEL   What's that bit for?

DAN   This bit?

RACHEL   Yes.

DAN   The ski-slots.

RACHEL   Where are the skis?

DAN   Um.
             They went.
             Somewhere.

RACHEL   Went.

DAN   But look!
             Ice-axe hook.
             Tool tubes
             Haul points.

RACHEL   Yes.

DAN	My goggles. With detachable, shatter-proof nose guard.
RACHEL	To prevent facial damage.
DAN	Yes.
RACHEL	When you fall.
DAN	If I fall.
RACHEL	Deflect the glare.
DAN	Of the sun.
RACHEL	The snow.
DAN	Exactly.
RACHEL	The UV rays.
DAN	We've got special sunscreen.
RACHEL	SPF 50.
DAN	Have to keep smearing it on.
RACHEL	The lips. The cheeks.
DAN	The nostrils.
RACHEL	Especially the nostrils.
DAN	They're prone to chapping. Rawness. Redness.
RACHEL	And you're how high?
DAN	Precisely eighteen thousand, two hundred feet.
RACHEL	It's virtually unscaled.
DAN	That's right.
RACHEL	It's highly dangerous. Inhospitable.
DAN	Yes.

RACHEL	But not if you have experience. Stamina. Fitness.
DAN	Which we do.
RACHEL	How's the air?
DAN	Thin.
RACHEL	How's the water?
DAN	Oh it's fine. There's loads.
RACHEL	Where do you keep it?
DAN	Here.
RACHEL	Doesn't look very big.
DAN	They're double-walled.
RACHEL	Yes.
DAN	Hot water, cold water.
RACHEL	Both.
DAN	And of course we've also got the stove.
RACHEL	The stove.
DAN	To melt the snow.
RACHEL	You're surrounded by snow.
DAN	You can eat the snow. If necessary.
RACHEL	A lot of snow is required to fully rehydrate the body.
DAN	But it's something. It's something.
RACHEL	If the stove breaks.
DAN	Which it won't.
RACHEL	If the stove breaks.

DAN   But you can always eat the snow.
           If you're desperate.

RACHEL   How long have you been sat there?

           Pause.

DAN   A few hours.
           A few days.

RACHEL   What's twelve times six?

DAN   Um?

RACHEL   Thirteen times thirty-seven.

DAN   Uh.

RACHEL   Eighty-eight divided by eighteen.

DAN   Okay, just hang on a minute!

RACHEL   Your body temperature is dropping
           dangerously low.
           Dan.

DAN   It's –
           No.

RACHEL   Symptoms of hypothermia include –

DAN   I'm wiggling my toes!

RACHEL   Irritability.
           Disorientation.
           Irrational behaviour.

DAN   No, look, see.
           Hello toes.
           One, two, three.
           Four, five…

RACHEL   You could take his jacket.

DAN   No.

RACHEL   He doesn't need it.

DAN   Yes he does.

RACHEL	Have you started eating the snow yet?
DAN	No.
RACHEL	If you're really desperate.
DAN	I'm not desperate. I'm just waiting.
RACHEL	For what?
DAN	For you.
RACHEL	But I'm not coming.
DAN	Yes you are.
RACHEL	I'm the one who's waiting…
DAN	You're coming to save me.
RACHEL	Like I always do.
DAN	It's like the story.
RACHEL	Haven't heard from you in three weeks. Dan.
DAN	The story. Rachel?
RACHEL	What story?
DAN	About Tam Lin.
RACHEL	I don't remember it.
DAN	Yes you do. *The Ballad of Tam Lin.*
RACHEL	How does it go?
DAN	You told it to me!
RACHEL	I don't remember.
DAN	Come on. You're obsessed with it! Janet, your favourite, she saves him. Janet saves Tam Lin. From the curse.

She holds fast, that's what she does.
She holds fast and saves him.

Silence.

She saves him, Rachel.

RACHEL *just looks at him.*

RACHEL.

2

DAN *and* RACHEL.

Just before the last trip.

DAN *is packing.*

RACHEL	It's like you're going off to war or something. All this stuff.
DAN	All necessary stuff.
RACHEL	Even this.
DAN	Especially that. Careful.
RACHEL	Tell me how high it is again?
DAN	Eighteen thousand, two hundred feet.
RACHEL	Right.
DAN	That's the summit elevation.
RACHEL	And the whole thing should take –
DAN	Between two to three weeks.
RACHEL	But probably three.
DAN	Depending on weather.
RACHEL	Probably three depending on weather.
DAN	That's right.

RACHEL   Dan.

DAN   What?

RACHEL   You're not wearing it.

Pause.

The St Christopher.

Pause.

DAN   Aren't I?

RACHEL   No.

Pause.

Have you lost it?

DAN   No.

RACHEL   You haven't.

DAN   I just…
Haven't worn it for a while.

RACHEL   Okay.

DAN   Cos I've been…
Well.
I've been here.

Pause.

RACHEL   But you're taking it with you.

DAN   Um.

RACHEL   Or aren't you?

DAN   No I am.

RACHEL   Okay.

DAN   But you know…!
I have to be a bit careful.

RACHEL   About?

DAN   I can't start –
Relying on stuff like that.
Thinking it'll save me.

RACHEL   It's just a bit of superstition.

DAN   I know.

RACHEL   Sentimentality.

DAN   Well.
         For who?

RACHEL   Okay.
           Yes.
           For me.

           Pause.

DAN   You know I don't go out there and think about –
        God.
        Or anything like that.

RACHEL   Okay.

DAN   It's not cos I want to commune with some kind
        of –
        Higher Power.

RACHEL   Then what is it about?

           Pause.

           What makes you want to do this?
           Climb things?

           Pause.

DAN   It's just…
        What I've always done.

RACHEL   You and Will.

DAN   Yes.

RACHEL   Didn't you say…
           That it was something inside you.
           Something frightening.

DAN   What?

RACHEL   You did.

DAN   No.
           No.
           It's just…
           Exhilaration.

RACHEL   Exertion.

DAN   Yes.

RACHEL   The thrill of it.

DAN   Exactly.

RACHEL   You know it's bad luck.

DAN   What is?

RACHEL   To lose a St Christopher.

DAN   I haven't lost it.
           I just…
           Once I've got this all done I'll get it out again
           and…

RACHEL   It's alright.

DAN   Of course I will –

RACHEL   It's just a story.
           Like you said.
           A story I tell myself.
           To make me feel better.

DAN   It's a nice story.

RACHEL   But that's all it is.
           I know that.

 # 3

WILL *and* DAN.

Just before the last trip.

There are maps spread out on the floor in front of them.

WILL *is drinking a beer.*

DAN *isn't.*

DAN	The sun sets around six o'clock.
WILL	Yep.
DAN	So we'll need to get up when the sun rises.
WILL	Of course.
DAN	We'll aim for eight hours' climbing a day. And at least seven hours' sleep a night.
WILL	That's not enough.
DAN	No?
WILL	Eight hours. Even nine.
DAN	We'll aim for eight hours' sleep.
WILL	Fine.
DAN	Good.
	Pause.
WILL	Have you missed it? Dan?
DAN	Pass me that map, would you?
WILL	I have.
DAN	I'm a bit concerned about the time of year.
WILL	Want to know what I've missed the most?
DAN	It will be icy. We're going to be exposed.

WILL	The dreams. I have the sexiest, filthiest, most depraved dreams you can imagine.
	Pause.
DAN	I know. You tell me about them. In great detail.
WILL	I'm a visionary. They're visions of the things to come.
DAN	It's the altitude. Nothing special.
WILL	Prude.
DAN	Doesn't affect me.
WILL	Of course it doesn't. Made of stone, you are.
DAN	Had enough beer have you?
	Pause.
WILL	Why? Do you want one?
DAN	No thanks.
WILL	You old woman.
DAN	We're leaving in two weeks.
WILL	I know. Three beers. Living life on the edge.
DAN	How many beers are there in your fridge, Will?
WILL	Yes so what's your point?
DAN	Three beers?
WILL	Yes okay.
	Pause.
DAN	We've got to fucking nail this.

WILL	I know that.
DAN	We're not eighteen any more.
WILL	Great-aunt Dan.
DAN	Not as photogenic as we used to be.
WILL	I like to think I've improved with age.
DAN	You haven't.
WILL	You definitely haven't.
DAN	If we fuck this up it's going to look pretty shabby.
WILL	Couldn't agree more. There's a lot of people invested in this.
DAN	Well, yes.
WILL	Who've placed a lot of trust in me.
DAN	In us.
WILL	Well. In me.
DAN	Been shagging them, have you?
WILL	Sometimes that's the only way to get the big bucks.
DAN	Whatever it takes, Will.
WILL	I've been working pretty hard on that particular front. Actually.

Pause.

DAN	We stick to the things we're good at. That's your area.
WILL	What? Fucking people?
DAN	So to speak.

They look at each other.

They look away.

WILL	And it worked, didn't it. We got the money.
DAN	We got the money.
WILL	Or – I got the money. For us.
	Pause.
DAN	Fine. Give me a beer.
WILL	That's more like it.
	Pause.
	They drink.
DAN	Remember Canada?
WILL	Yeah.
DAN	Me dangling off that rock face.
WILL	Course.
DAN	Thought that was it.
WILL	Nah. I was there.
DAN	Took you a while.
WILL	Still.
DAN	Thought I was going to shit myself.
WILL	I know. You told me. I thought, shit, if he shits himself, what's it going to land on? Or who?
DAN	Thought crossed my mind too.
WILL	That's what spurred me into action.
DAN	Finally.

WILL	I mustered my last ounce of strength and hauled you back.
DAN	Two hours later.
WILL	Fat bastard.
DAN	You puked as I remember.
WILL	On your boots.
DAN	Yep.
WILL	You were really upset about your boots.
DAN	They were bloody expensive.
WILL	You were more upset about your boots than a plunge to certain death chased by your own shit.
DAN	Still annoyed you puked on my boots.

Pause.

We're up to this.
Aren't we?

WILL	You and me? Invincible.
DAN	You think so?
WILL	I'm still fit as a fiddle.
DAN	So am I.
WILL	Fitter than you.
DAN	We'll see.
WILL	You'd better not be chickening out on me.
DAN	Never.
WILL	If there's any part of you that isn't up for this –
DAN	I'm up for this.
WILL	Met a guy in Germany last year. Called Lars. Norwegian guy.

> Not much fun, but he'd get it done, you know.
> He'd definitely get it done.

DAN   I'm in.

WILL   So will you trust me?

DAN   I suppose so.

WILL   Will you trust me?

DAN   Yes.
        Yes.

WILL   Excellent.
         I know you'd come round.
         You old woman.

4

Before.

A party.

It's loud.

RACHEL, WILL *and* DAN *are awkwardly thrown together.*

Mid-conversation.

RACHEL   I'm basically a massive spod.

WILL   What?

RACHEL   I said I'm a massive SPOD.

WILL   Sexy.

RACHEL   Yeah!

         They nod at each other, smiling.

         Okay, well strictly I'm *applying* for a PhD...
         I just have to get funding, which means a million
         interviews and letters and being rejected, and

	getting angry, but then hopefully maybe eventually – I will be doing a PhD.
DAN	What's your subject?
WILL	Oh here he is! Piping up!
RACHEL	Oh um. Well it's interesting you should ask actually cos it's – It's kind of hard to – Well part of the problem is that it's really, really massive and – It sort of keeps growing and growing which is a bit – Worrying? Anyway. The short version is that it's about folk songs and war and women. And Empire and being English. Oh and movement. Travel. Acquisitiveness. But the urge to keep moving in particular. Put distance behind you. Cos I might also look at the Romantic era. The poets. They're all about escape. But that might be something else. I don't know. But I could weave it in maybe…? I'm hoping I can weave it in. Does that make sense? It doesn't, does it? God no wonder no one will give me any money.
DAN	I, I think it makes sense.
WILL	He doesn't know what half those words mean!
RACHEL	Do you? Do you really?

WILL	Dan had to retake his GCSE Geography. How many times was it, Dan?
DAN	No I didn't.
WILL	Which is a bit ironic actually. Considering what we do now.
RACHEL	Why? What do you do now?
WILL	Guess.
RACHEL	God, I don't know. You work for one of those really obnoxious management consultancies.
WILL	What?!
RACHEL	You're in financial PR.
WILL	You're offending my manhood, here.
RACHEL	You're a stand-up comedian.
WILL	We're mountaineers.
RACHEL	What?
WILL	Adventurers. Explorers.
RACHEL	Are you? Are you really?
DAN	Only in a modest sense.
WILL	Modest?! What the fuck are you talking about, Dan? We climbed Everest when we were eighteen!
RACHEL	You did not.
WILL	Yes we fucking did.
RACHEL	That's – Simply ridiculous.
WILL	We were in all the papers.
DAN	Some of the papers.

WILL	Bet you saw us. I had this really great jacket. Dan looked a bit weird…
RACHEL	How do you even start to make that the thing you do?
WILL	By being exceptional.
RACHEL	At what?
WILL	Life.
RACHEL	Don't you need a lot of money?
DAN	Yes.
RACHEL	Ah-ha.
WILL	That's such an unromantic way to look at it!
DAN	You need a lot of money.
WILL	There's so much money in the world! You just have to find a way to get it to flow towards you.
RACHEL	I'm not sure I agree with that. In fact I think I quite strenuously disagree with that.
WILL	Oh I'm sorry. I must have misheard you earlier.
RACHEL	When?
WILL	A million interviews, letters, rejections, getting angry.
RACHEL	Yes but that's –
WILL	What?
RACHEL	Different.
WILL	How?
RACHEL	They're two completely different things!
WILL	There's probably all sorts of blood on that respectable PhD money.

RACHEL   And anyway.
          Are you actually doing anything to help preserve
          the land you're trampling all over?
          Or are you just contributing to its destruction?

DAN   We do raise quite a bit of money for charity
          actually…

RACHEL   Oh.
          Well I suppose that's quite admirable.

WILL   Careful!
          You'll give yourself a heart attack with that kind
          of enthusiasm.

RACHEL   But it's just all a bit English isn't it?

WILL   English?!

DAN   What do you mean?

RACHEL   You just want to stick flags on virgin territory and
          claim it as your own.
          God it's pretty phallic actually.
          I mean, for example.
          In these folk songs.
          There's always a man.
          Going off to war, in a ship.
          In a uniform.
          And there's a woman, often called Nancy.
          Nancy is on the dock, looking nice, waving
          a handkerchief.
          And she says, hang on, can't I just come with you?
          Why can't I put on the uniform?
          I could dress up like a man, cut off all my hair.
          And the man is like –
          'Oh Nancy!
          Beautiful Nancy!
          NO!
          Your waist is too narrow!
          Your shoulders are too small.'
          Nancy would just cramp his style.
          He just wants to get on with his raping and
          pillaging unrumbled.

He just wants to wear his enormous hat.
Brandish his massive musket and fill jam jars with
misshapen fetuses that he's probably ripped from
some indigenous woman's womb.
Maybe do some experiments on her skull.
Bring a few diseases into the mix, why not?
Sprinkle some poxes and fevers around.
Kill off a few innocuous people.
Innocent people, people who never asked to be
discovered, to be civilised, to be *wiped out* by
arrogant, cruel, wicked people in hats and medals
who dare to impose their religion, their belief
system, their entire way of life and anyway.
I'm ranting.
Aren't I?
I'm not suggesting that's what you do, I'm just
making an analogy.
Sorry.

Silence.

WILL   I'm going to buy you a drink.

RACHEL   Are you?

WILL   And then...

RACHEL   Then...?

WILL   I'm going to take you into that corner over there.
I'm going to look at you.
So that you get dizzy.
And I'm going to kiss you for a very, very
long time.

Silence.

So I'm just letting you know.

RACHEL   Okay.
Um.
Good.

WILL stands up.

WILL   Don't let her go anywhere.

WILL exits.

DAN and RACHEL look at each other.

Then look away.

Then back again.

RACHEL   So he's...
         Wow.
         He's quite...

DAN   Oh.
         He's alright.

         Silence.

         The thing is...
         Sometimes it's almost like a...
         Like a sickness.

RACHEL   What is?

DAN   Like you can't stop.
         You want to stop.
         But you can't.
         You have to go higher.
         Cos the higher you are, the safer you feel...

RACHEL   Why?

DAN   I don't know.
         It's just something inside you.
         Making you do it.
         Something a bit –
         A bit frightening.

         They look at each other.

         WILL returns.

WILL   Here you go.

RACHEL   What is that?

WILL   Vodka.
         Lime.
         Soda.

RACHEL	Pah, I don't drink vodka.
WILL	Well I'm not getting you another one.
RACHEL	Bet you will.
WILL	I bloody won't.
RACHEL	I'm Rachel, by the way. What's your name?

5

WILL *and* DAN.

The mountain.

A few days into the climb.

WILL	I need to piss.
DAN	Again?
WILL	Look don't make a comment. You don't have to make a comment every time.
DAN	Well hurry up.
WILL	I am.
DAN	Come on.
WILL	I am.
	Pause.
DAN	You look a bit fucked.
WILL	What?
DAN	You okay?
WILL	Course.
DAN	You just look a bit fucked that's all.
WILL	Such an old woman.

DAN   You sure you're alright?

WILL   Yes!
           Yes.

           Pause.

           DAN *reaches for something around his neck.*

           WILL *watches him.*

           What is that thing?

DAN   What?

WILL   That thing you wear around your neck.

DAN   Oh.
           It's –

           He grips the St Christopher.

           He lets it go.

           Nothing special.

           Pause.

WILL   You hold on to it a lot.

DAN   What?

WILL   You hold on to the pendant bit.

           DAN*'s hand flies up to the St Christopher.*

           He stops himself from holding it.

DAN   No I don't.

WILL   Someone give it to you?

           Pause.

           That's nice.
           Cares about you.

DAN   Oh…

WILL   Wants to keep you safe.

DAN   Don't know why I wear it really.
           I mean it's a piece of tin.

	Look at it. Pointless.
WILL	It's more than that isn't it?
DAN	Not a big deal. Whatever.
WILL	You're lucky, Dan.
DAN	It's nothing.
WILL	Don't piss on it.
	Pause.
DAN	Here.
WILL	What?
DAN	You take it.
WILL	Don't be a prick.
DAN	I'm serious.
WILL	Do you know what that thing means?
DAN	It doesn't mean anything! It's... it's fantasy!
WILL	Then why do you want to give it to me?
DAN	Because I –
WILL	Do you think I need it more than you?
DAN	No –
WILL	Because that's bollocks and you know it.
	Pause.
	Keep hold of that thing.
DAN	What's got into you?
WILL	It's bad luck.
DAN	What is?
WILL	She didn't give it to me.
DAN	No I know.

WILL	Keep hold of it.
	Promise me?

| DAN | Okay I get it. |

WILL	Whatever happens you hang on to that.
	Okay?
	Promise, Dan?

Pause.

| DAN | I promise. |

6

WILL *and* RACHEL.

A hill in Wales.

They are kissing.

Passionately.

WILL	Wait!

| RACHEL | What? |

| WILL | I want you to commune with my homeland! |

| RACHEL | I am. |
| | It's lovely. |

They keep kissing.

| WILL | You have no interest in my place of birth! |
| | My formative years! |

| RACHEL | I really, really do. |

They keep kissing.

| WILL | You appear to be trying to distract me. |

| RACHEL | From what? |

| WILL | From the edge. |

RACHEL   Now why would I do that?

WILL   We are very, very high up you know…

RACHEL   I'll stand on the edge.
           Look!

WILL   That is so not the edge.

RACHEL   Okay.
           Okay but this is.
           Right?

WILL   Look down.

RACHEL   What?

WILL   Look down.

RACHEL   No!

WILL   Go on.
           Looking down is the best bit.

RACHEL   You look down.

WILL   Okay fine.

           Beat.

RACHEL   Stop!

WILL   Why?

RACHEL   You'll fall…

WILL   Well, I might…
           If I did this.

RACHEL   Gah, I'm not watching!

WILL   Or this?

RACHEL   Don't!!

WILL   Come on!
           Come here.

           Pause.

           Look, you can see where we're staying.
           See?

RACHEL   Oh yeah...
            It looks a lot prettier from up here cos you can't
            see the Costcutter.

            They look.

WILL   Go on.
            Tell me it isn't beautiful.

RACHEL   It's beautiful.

WILL   No, but have a proper reaction.

RACHEL   It's... it's amazing.
            Glorious.

WILL   You're not looking properly.

RACHEL   You're distracting me.
            I can't concentrate.

WILL   Why?
            Cos you like me?

RACHEL   No.
            I don't like you at all.

WILL   I don't like you either.
            You're awful.

RACHEL   You're terrible.
            Really unattractive.

WILL   Are you having a terrible time?

RACHEL   This whole trip has just been really terrible.

WILL   I wish I wasn't standing on this hilltop with you
            at dusk.
            The whole of Wales at my feet.
            Wine in my backpack.
            About to sup it from tiny plastic beakers.

RACHEL   You –
            You brought wine?

WILL   I did.

            Pause.

RACHEL   I mean, I'm still pretty pissed.
           From all the whisky...

WILL   Yes but this is wine, Rachel.
           It's a completely different olfactory experience.

RACHEL   I think I'm still hungover from yesterday...

WILL   Red or white?

RACHEL   Red OR white?

WILL   I know how to treat a lady.

RACHEL   God.
           I don't know.
           White?

WILL   An excellent choice

           He hands RACHEL *a plastic beaker of wine.*

           They cheers – in Welsh perhaps.

           They drink.

RACHEL   Well that was an interesting definition of an
           evening stroll.

WILL   Oh we're not done yet.
           This isn't the bit.

RACHEL   This *isn't* the bit?

WILL   No, no, no.
           We've got to get to the waterfall.

RACHEL   There's a waterfall?

WILL   Yes.

RACHEL   You didn't mention a waterfall.

WILL   Of course I did!
           That's the whole reason we're here.

RACHEL   Well, how much further is it?

WILL   Oh it's close.

RACHEL   Will.

WILL	About forty-five minutes.
RACHEL	How much?
WILL	To an hour.
RACHEL	You said we'd only be gone thirty minutes!
WILL	No... Did I?
RACHEL	I was about to get in the bath!
WILL	No more baths. A person can die taking so many baths.
RACHEL	But I'm... I'm knackered!
WILL	You just need a quick rest.
RACHEL	Couldn't we just have done this tomorrow? In daylight?
WILL	This is daylight!
RACHEL	Barely.
WILL	Where's your sense of adventure?
RACHEL	My sense of adventure is fine. I just want to, you know... Indulge it back at the hotel.
WILL	Rachel –
RACHEL	You said a quick stroll after dinner. And suddenly there's a waterfall...
WILL	This place is important to me, you know.
RACHEL	Okay –
WILL	I thought you'd love it.
RACHEL	I told you it was beautiful!
WILL	But you didn't mean it enough.
RACHEL	Will, I'm tired. Can we please just go back.

WILL   No.

RACHEL   What do you mean, no?

WILL   We're having a brilliant time.

RACHEL   You might be.
            I'm not.

WILL   I'm going to make you have a brilliant time.

RACHEL   I don't think it works like that –

WILL   Well I'm going to MAKE it work like that.

            WILL *downs the entire bottle of wine.*

            Silence.

            Right.
            I'm going to go up there.

RACHEL   Sorry –
            Where?

WILL   This path.
            I am going to follow it.

RACHEL   I see.
            This path.
            That is leading.
            Uphill.

WILL   Yes.

RACHEL   Why?

WILL   Cos I want to.
            I have an urge.

RACHEL   You can't go up there.

WILL   Yes I can.

RACHEL   You cannot.

WILL   Indeed I can.
            And I shall.

RACHEL   Fine.
          You'll be going by yourself then.

WILL   Yup.

RACHEL   Cos I'm not coming with you.

WILL   Fine by me.

RACHEL   Well then.
          Off you go.

WILL   See you back at the hotel for sherry hour.

RACHEL   Yep.

WILL   May I offer you the torch?

RACHEL   Nope.
          Don't need it.

WILL   Okeedokee.

RACHEL   Catch you later.

WILL   Toodle pip.

RACHEL   Yep.
          BYE.

          WILL *exits*.

          Silence.

          Will?
          Will?

          Silence.

          WILL, COME BACK YOU FUCKING
          BASTARD.

#7

RACHEL *and* DAN.

Night.

DAN *wakes with a start.*

He sits up suddenly.

He rubs his eyes.

He puts his head in his hands.

RACHEL *stirs.*

RACHEL   Hey…

        Nothing.

        You okay?

        DAN *tries to breathe.*

        She sits up and leans against him.

        Silence.

DAN   Sorry.

RACHEL   It's okay…

DAN   No, I'm really…

RACHEL   Shh…
It's alright.

        Silence.

DAN   I'm…
I'm in such a muddle.

RACHEL   It's okay.

DAN   I don't know what's the matter with me, I'm…

RACHEL   Shh…

DAN   I can't breathe.

RACHEL   Yes you can.
You can.
Come on.

They breathe.

Shall I open the window?

He doesn't answer.

Dan?

He doesn't answer.

I'll open the window a bit.

DAN   I think I'm dying.

RACHEL   No.

DAN   Yes.

RACHEL   It's alright –

DAN   My heart is about to stop.

RACHEL   No.

DAN   Yes.
             One more beat.
             Maybe two.
             Then that –
             Will be that.

RACHEL   Your heart is fine.
             See?

             She puts her hand on his heart.

             See?

             He tries to breathe.

             They are quiet.

             I'm going to get you some water.

DAN   Don't go.

RACHEL   Dan –

DAN   Don't.
             Stay.
             Please.

             Silence.

RACHEL   Better?

Silence.

DAN   No.
No.
Worse.

He sits up suddenly.

I've got to…
Get out of here.

He stands up.

I can't stay in here it's too…
It's too hot.

RACHEL   Dan.

DAN   Why is it so hot in here?

RACHEL   Just wait for a second.

DAN   I just have to –
I just have to WALK.

RACHEL   Okay.

DAN   It's all this being still, it's too…
It's like a fucking noose, I can't…

RACHEL   Please just sit down.

DAN   Don't touch me.

RACHEL   Dan –

DAN   Don't TOUCH me.

Silence.

RACHEL   Okay fine.
You want to go?
Go.

DAN is piling on clothes.

Go and get mown down by a drunk driver.
I don't care any more, Dan.
Be my guest.

DAN is about to leave.

He turns round and looks at her.

DAN   I've always been very clear.
      That this is the deal.

RACHEL   What is the 'deal' exactly?

DAN   I told you.
      I can't just sit around and stagnate, it's just not
      an option for me –

RACHEL   It was your choice.
         You chose this.

DAN   No I did not.

RACHEL   What?

DAN   You chose this.
      For me.

RACHEL   I –
         Can't believe you would say that.

DAN   I gave up all of that.
      The things I love.
      My *identity*.
      For you.

RACHEL   Wow.
         Okay.

DAN   That's what I did, Rachel.

RACHEL   No.
         Don't do this.

DAN   Do what?!

RACHEL   You said you were done with it all.
         That is what you said.

DAN   I never said that.

RACHEL   Oh my God.

DAN   When did I say that?

RACHEL   Don't you dare.

DAN   Rachel.
           Tell me when I said that.

RACHEL   Don't you dare start rewriting everything.

           He turns away from her.

           She watches him.

           It scares me.

           He is still turned away from her.

           Whose version is going to last, Dan?
           Yours or mine?

           Silence.

           What do you think history teaches us about whose
           version is going to last?

           He is ready to leave.

           He looks back at her briefly.

DAN   I'll be back, I don't know…
           Soon.

           Silence.

RACHEL   Just go.

           They stare at each other.

           GO.

8

The present.

The mountain.

WILL	Dan. Dan.
DAN	What?
WILL	This isn't the way.
	DAN *ignores him.*
	Dan.
	DAN *ignores him.*
	Will you listen to me?
DAN	I'm in a rhythm.
WILL	DAN. Stop.
	DAN *stops.*
	Something's wrong.
DAN	What do you mean?
	Pause.
	What do you mean, Will?
WILL	I just want to stop for a minute okay?
DAN	It's... it's all going to plan. We're fine.
WILL	I just need to – Focus for a minute.
	Silence.
DAN	How long is this little existential crisis going to last?
WILL	Can you just give me a fucking second here?
	Pause.
	I feel a bit – Dizzy.

DAN   Okay.
         Drink some water.
         Go on.

WILL   I don't feel like it.

DAN   Come on.
         You'll feel better for a bit of water.

WILL   No.

DAN   Listen.
         I think there's going to be a white-out.
         We've got to keep moving.
         We have to get to that bit of shelter up ahead.
         Like we talked about.
         Okay?

         Silence.

         We're too exposed here.
         You know that.

WILL   We've gone wrong.

DAN   We –
         We haven't.

WILL   Something isn't right.

DAN   Just have some water.

WILL   I have a bad feeling.

DAN   Well –
         Well that's all it is.
         A feeling.

         Pause.

WILL   Okay.
         I've decided.

DAN   What?

WILL   We're going back down.

DAN   Don't be stupid.

WILL   We've got to get back to where we first went
                wrong.

DAN   We haven't gone wrong.

WILL   I'm going back down even if you're not.

DAN   Will.
                No.

WILL   I'm telling you something's wrong.

DAN   Yes.
                Something is wrong.
                With you.

WILL   With me?

DAN   You're not fit enough.

WILL   Excuse me?

DAN   You didn't take it seriously.
                And now look at you.

WILL   You're not hearing me.

DAN   I knew this would happen.

WILL   Listen to me.

DAN   I fucking knew it.

WILL   LISTEN to me.
                We have gone very very wrong.
                And we are going to die if we don't turn round.
                And go back down.
                Now.

                Pause.

                Where are you going?

DAN   I'm not listening to this.

WILL   Dan.

DAN   The only thing that's 'gone wrong' is us standing
                here discussing the meaning of life.

WILL	You're a cold bastard aren't you?
DAN	Yeah well if I wasn't you'd be dead.
	Silence.
WILL	Give me the water.
DAN	Okay. Good.
	WILL *starts tipping the water away.*
	What… What are you doing?
WILL	Listen to me, Dan. We need to go back down.
DAN	What the fuck are you doing?
WILL	Are you going to listen to me? Are you?
DAN	It – It doesn't matter. We can just melt some more snow. You can't intimidate me.
WILL	Stove's on its last legs.
DAN	No it isn't. What?
WILL	Didn't want to tell you. Bum you out. But it's not in the best shape.
	He continues pouring away the water.
DAN	You're a liability, you know that? You're a fucking psycho.
WILL	We're going back down. Okay, Dan? That's what we're going to do.
DAN	You wouldn't really. You wouldn't.

WILL *tilts the flask at a more extreme angle.*

Water gushes out.

You've actually gone crazy.

WILL   Not much left now, Dan.
So are we going down or what?

DAN   I –

WILL *turns the flask completely upside down.*

Okay!
Okay.
Whatever you say.
Whatever you think is best, Will.
I'm listening.

WILL   Good.

 # 9

RACHEL, DAN *and* WILL.

Before.

WILL *has his head in* RACHEL*'s lap.*

RACHEL   So Tam Lin is a musician.
A wandering minstrel.
He's been captured by the Queen of the Fairies –
Do you really want to hear about this?

DAN   No.
Please.
I want to hear it.

RACHEL   So.
She's beautiful –
Of course.
But she's a monster.

WILL   Rachel?

RACHEL   She's cursed him.
            Every seven years, Tam Lin has to make a tithe
            to Hell.
            Which means he has to die so the Queen can have
            eternal life.

WILL   Why aren't you lavishing me with attention?
            It's my birthday.

RACHEL   Tam Lin guards the path to Carterhaugh.
            And every time a woman passes, he has to bar
            their path.
            Demand what it is they're doing in these lands.

WILL   It just seems extraordinary to me.
            That I am not being kissed at this very moment.

RACHEL   And he has to rape them.

DAN   What?

RACHEL   Yes.
            It's all part of the curse.
            Maybe it's her revenge on all the beautiful young
            women.
            Who knows?
            But then Janet comes along.
            She wears her skirt hitched up to her knees and
            a green mantle.
            She's great!
            She doesn't need anyone!
            But she takes one look at Tam and falls madly in
            love with him.
            Because that's what happens.

WILL   You know how much I hate not having any
            attention.

DAN   So he doesn't rape her.

RACHEL   Oh yes.
            He does.

DAN   He does?

RACHEL   And then she's pregnant.
           Her father is furious.
           He gives her a herb which will kill the unborn
           child inside her.
           But she refuses to take it.
           She's having that baby cos it's Tam Lin's.
           She makes it her mission to rescue him from the
           clutches of the evil Queen.

DAN   How does she do that?

RACHEL   She has to just hold on to him.

DAN   What do you mean?

RACHEL   Well.
           The Queen turns him into a million weird things.
           An eel, a lion, a naked knight.
           But she has to just hold on.
           To her One True Love.

DAN   And does she?

RACHEL   She does.
           Yes.
           She saves him.

WILL   You two are really pissing me off.

           DAN *and* RACHEL *look at* WILL.

           Silence.

           They look at each other.

           Why are you looking at each other like that?

RACHEL   We –
           We weren't.

DAN   We weren't.

           WILL *looks at them.*

WILL   You think I'm drunk.

RACHEL   No.

DAN   No.

RACHEL   It's your birthday...

DAN   Happy birthday, mate...!

WILL   Stop looking at me like that.

RACHEL and DAN look away.

Stop doing everything I say.

They look back at him.

Can I speak to my girlfriend for a minute?
Mate.

Pause.

DAN *stands up.*

He moves away from them.

He keeps watching them.

WILL *takes RACHEL's hand.*

I don't deserve.
To be laughed at.

RACHEL   No one's laughing at you –

WILL   Let me finish.

Pause.

RACHEL *glances at DAN.*

No don't look at him.

RACHEL   I wasn't.

Pause.

WILL   I'd like you to see me.

RACHEL   Okay.

She looks at him.

What do you want me to see?

WILL   The truth.

RACHEL   What is that?

WILL	That I'm a fucking… Superhero.
	RACHEL *glances at* DAN.
	Aren't I?
RACHEL	Yes.
WILL	Don't humour me.
RACHEL	I'm not –
WILL	Why are you always looking at him?
	Pause.
	Why?
RACHEL	Will. You're hurting my –
WILL	Why?
DAN	Will, mate. Let go of her.
WILL	What do I have to do? To get you to see me?
DAN	Come on. Let's go for a walk around the block, or…?
WILL	Once, just once. I'd like you to say – You know what, Will?
DAN	Come on, mate.
WILL	You've done some amazing things.
RACHEL	You've done some amazing things.
WILL	You're a pretty awesome guy.
RACHEL	You're…
WILL	Say it.
DAN	Will, let's just –
WILL	I was in all the papers.

RACHEL   Yes.

DAN   Let's get you some water or –

WILL   Wasn't I?

RACHEL   You were.

WILL   But still.
You're leaving.

RACHEL   Will…

WILL   Do you know how many miles Boston is from here?

RACHEL   Not off the top of my head.

WILL   Three thousand, two hundred and sixty-nine.

RACHEL   That doesn't have anything to do with –

WILL   What?

RACHEL   To do with you.

WILL   That.
Is exactly my point.

He looks at DAN.

He waits for DAN *to say something that will make him feel better.*

DAN *doesn't.*

All my life, you know…
I only had to shit and someone would applaud me.

DAN   Will –

WILL   But it doesn't mean anything.
The only person it would mean anything from is going to the other side of the world to get away from me.
The only person it would mean anything from thinks I'm worth nothing.

He lets go of her hand.

And she's probably right.
She's right.

WILL stands up.

He sits at the edge of the stage.

RACHEL and DAN look at each other.

For a long time.

She looks at WILL.

She looks back at DAN.

RACHEL   Who started it?

DAN   What?

RACHEL   Do you remember?

They look at each other.

It was you.

DAN   Was it?

RACHEL   You leaned over and...

DAN   No...?

RACHEL   Yes.
You were holding something.

DAN   Yes...

RACHEL   Yes.

They look at each other.

DAN leans closer to RACHEL.

DAN   I actually...
I got you something.

RACHEL   Did you...?

DAN   Yeah kind of a...
Going away.
Thing.
Gift.

He hands her a gift.

She looks at it.

She looks at him.

Go on.
Open it.

Slowly, she opens it.

She looks at it.

You see…
You see there's this bookshop near mine
I walk past it most days but I…
I never go in.
And the other day I just thought…
Why don't I ever go in there!?

RACHEL   Dan –

DAN   So I did.
           There aren't even any proper shelves.
           The books are all just piled up on the floor.
           You kind of have to weave your way through them
           and you're worried you'll knock them over.

RACHEL   This is…

DAN   And I just thought, I wonder if they'll have
           anything…
           And, and turned out…
           There was that.
           So.

           Pause.

           It's probably not an actual first edition.

RACHEL   It's a first – ?

DAN   Well, it says it is, if you look…

           RACHEL *looks.*

RACHEL   I don't quite know what to…

DAN   But you like it…?
             Do you?

             She looks at him.

RACHEL   Thank you.

DAN   Yeah?

RACHEL   Yes.
             Yes.

             They look at each other.

             DAN *leans in even closer.*

DAN   I just feel like.
             Like this is really important.

RACHEL   Yes.

DAN   Cos I'm making a choice.
             Aren't I?

             He looks at WILL.

             And I think…
             In fact I know.
             That I'm making the right one.

RACHEL   Doesn't make it any easier.

DAN   No.

RACHEL   But in many ways…
             The choice was kind of…
             It was kind of made for us.

DAN   In many ways we didn't have a choice.

RACHEL   Yes.
             Yes?

DAN   Yes –

             She leans over and kisses him.

 # 10

DAN *and* RACHEL.

A few weeks later.

Early morning.

WILL *is still watching them.*

They look at WILL *warily.*

They look at each other.

After a moment they smile.

Alone together.

RACHEL   I have to get up soon…

DAN   Do you?

She doesn't get up.

RACHEL   Or I could just stay here…

DAN   All day…?

RACHEL   Hmm.
Possibly…

DAN   All day.

RACHEL   Well, I'm not making any promises…

DAN   I'll bring you tea.

RACHEL   I think…
You might make the worst tea I've ever drunk.

DAN   Do I?

RACHEL   You really do.

DAN   What's so bad about it?!

RACHEL   It's got those bits floating in it.
Scummy bits.

DAN   It doesn't!

RACHEL   You get the tea-to-milk ratio all wrong.

DAN   What?!

RACHEL   But I still drink it...

         Pause.

         I mean, I have to pack.

DAN   You're not leaving for another month.

RACHEL   I have to read about twenty-seven different books.
         Which all have about eight hundred pages.
         A month...
         God.

         They look at each other.

DAN   Yeah.

RACHEL   You'll be busy.
         Preparing.

DAN   I will.

RACHEL   And I mean, they actually have phones and
         internet and –
         General civilisation.
         Where I'm going.

DAN   Yes.

RACHEL   Whereas you and Will are...
         Off into the wilderness.
         Again.

         Pause.

RACHEL   I got you something.

DAN   Did you?

RACHEL   Here.

         She holds out the St Christopher.

         DAN *takes it.*

         He's the patron saint of travel or something.
         St Christopher is.
         It keeps you safe.

DAN *looks at it.*

I mean.
It doesn't.
But it's quite a nice story.

DAN   Yes.

RACHEL   You don't have to actually wear it.
               You can put it in a drawer and forget about it if
               you –

DAN puts it on.

DAN   Look.
               You've turned me into a wearer of lucky charms.

RACHEL   Or you could just not go.
               Couldn't you?

Silence.

RACHEL looks confused.

She looks at WILL, as if for confirmation.

That's…
I don't know what just happened there.

DAN   What did you just ask?

RACHEL   Nothing.
               I didn't.

DAN   Is that what you want?

RACHEL   No.
               No, it's not.

They look at each other.

Neither of them quite seems sure what to do.

DAN   What if I stayed?

RACHEL   I don't want you to stay.
               I don't.
               That's stupid.

DAN   And what if you stayed?

RACHEL	No. No, I'm going to Boston.
DAN	You are.
RACHEL	Of course. It's an incredible opportunity.
DAN	What you've always dreamed of.
RACHEL	And you're going to Peru. With Will. Been talking about it since you were, what?
DAN	Nineteen. Twenty?
RACHEL	You've spent months planning it.
DAN	And you – You've worked really hard.
RACHEL	I've worked my arse off, to be fair.
DAN	But the thing is…
RACHEL	Yes?
DAN	I've been thinking…
RACHEL	Yes…?
DAN	I have been thinking…
	Pause.
	That if you go. And I go.
RACHEL	Yes.
DAN	Well, then, that's kind of… The end. Of this.
RACHEL	Yes
DAN	Is that what we both…?
RACHEL	I don't know…

DAN   I mean, it's not what I…

RACHEL   No?

DAN   Is it what you…?

             Pause.

RACHEL   Have you…
             Spoken to him?

             Pause.

DAN   You know.
             He takes a lot of risks…
             Out there.

             She waits.

             Once we had to wait all night.
             In a hole scooped out of snow.
             Cos he said we didn't need headlamps.
             There was a blizzard and –
             He wanted to go ahead.
             In the dark.
             I almost had to hold him down to stop him from
             taking off.
             The next morning we tried to make it back and…
             I'd lost one of my skis.
             It was still snowing.
             I was crying, at one point, we were only, what,
             sixteen?
             Kids.
             It took hours…
             But we made it.
             When we got down it felt…

RACHEL   What?

DAN   Fucking amazing…

             Pause.

RACHEL   Dan.
             You'll be climbing the walls.

DAN   No.
             I want to be free of that.
             Him.

RACHEL   Do you?

DAN   He's pushed me around for too long, it's…
             I mean, he's pushed both of us around!

             Pause.

             There comes a point when you just.
             You've had enough.

             They look at each other.

             And I mean…
             This.
             Here.
             Is everything.

RACHEL   Everything…

DAN   I mean it.
             Right now I…
             I sort of don't give a shit about anything else.

             Pause.

RACHEL   We're saying dangerous things.

             They look at each other.

             Or maybe we just thought them…

             She looks at WILL.

             We didn't actually say those things out loud.
             Did we?
             We didn't.

11

WILL *and* RACHEL.

After DAN*'s departure.*

RACHEL   So he hasn't – ?

WILL   No.
          Sorry.

RACHEL   I just wondered if he might have come here.
          But.

WILL   Haven't heard from him in a while.

RACHEL   No?

WILL   Years.
          Actually.

          Pause.

WILL   So when did he –
          Take off?

RACHEL   Uh.
          A while ago.
          A few days.
          He's done it before.
          He just.
          He disappears.

WILL   Yes.

RACHEL   But never for long.
          I keep busy.

WILL   Do you?

RACHEL   And then I look up and he's –
          He's back.
          So.

          Silence.

          She looks around her.

          Why don't you have any furniture?

WILL   Well I've.
              Only just moved in.

RACHEL   You said you'd been here two months.

WILL   Exactly.
              Only just moved in.

              Pause.

              Actually it's a design choice.

RACHEL   You could at least…
              Put a shade over a bulb.
              Or something.

WILL   'Spartan Chic.'

RACHEL   What alcohol do you have?

              Pause.

WILL   I'm trying not to.

RACHEL   Oh.

WILL   Not for any…
              I mean, I'm just trying.
              For a bit.

RACHEL   Sorry.

WILL   No, no –

RACHEL   Sorry.

WILL   It's good to see you.

              Silence.

              You must be a doctor now.
              Dr Rachel.

RACHEL   Oh.
              Sort of.

WILL   Sort of?

RACHEL   I'm kind of behind.
              With all that.
              There were some setbacks.

WILL   But you're still…?

RACHEL   Oh yes.
            Absolutely.
            I have a deadline and it's –
            Totally on track…

WILL   Great.

RACHEL   That's a lie.

WILL   Thought it was.

RACHEL   Fuck.

            Pause.

WILL   I've been in Korea.

RACHEL   Really?

WILL   Teaching English.

RACHEL   And were you good at that?

WILL   I was fucking awful.

RACHEL   Yes I can imagine.

WILL   But it was weird cos –
            I had this apartment.
            With all this air conditioning.
            And cushions.
            And a housekeeper.

RACHEL   I see.

WILL   And she left little pots on my cooker with
            instructions.
            'Heat for forty minutes'.
            'Serve with sauce in pot in door of fridge'.

RACHEL   Sounds –

WILL   Fucking fantastic.

RACHEL   Yes.

WILL   But in the end it wasn't really worth it.
You know.
For a housekeeper.

Pause.

RACHEL   I never went to Boston.

WILL   I know.

RACHEL   Why didn't I?

WILL   I can't tell you that.

RACHEL   I'm a fool.

WILL   Perhaps.

RACHEL   And now here I am.
The anchor.
To his ship.

Pause.

Sometimes I tell myself…
That I'm going to go into a wood.
With a tent.
I'm going to live in the tent.
For months.
As many months as I can.
I'm going to learn about birds.
And snakes.
I'm going to learn about wood.
How to chop it, how to make fire from it.
I'm going to kill my own food.
I'll have a gun.
And a knife.
I'm going to grow my hair.
I'll have hair all over my body.
By the time I come back I'll be too old for people
to ask those questions of me.
When?
When will you tie yourself to him with a rope?
Relinquish your name?
Push out his child?

I'll be too old and withered for people to even
look at me much any more.
I won't even be visible.

WILL   Sounds like a nice fantasy.

RACHEL   It isn't a fantasy when *you* do it.

WILL   But that's not what I do.

RACHEL   No?

WILL   I have Dan.
Or I did…

Silence.

RACHEL   You're right.

WILL   Yes.

RACHEL   He's just…
Adrift.
Dan is.

WILL   Yes.

RACHEL   And he's not the only one.

WILL   I'm not.

RACHEL   Are you kidding?
You're the worst.

Pause.

What happened?

He turns away from her.

WILL   Maybe I…
I just don't expect as much from life as you do.

RACHEL   You used to want everything.

Pause.

You two should do another climb.
Together.

WILL   What?

RACHEL   You should.

           Pause.

           It might help.
           Both of you.

WILL   Who says I need help?

RACHEL   Him then.
           It might help him.

WILL   I don't think so, Rachel.

RACHEL   Why not?

WILL   There are a million reasons why I wouldn't…
           No.
           It's just too…

RACHEL   I think it's a good idea.

WILL   No.
           No chance.

RACHEL   Think about it.

WILL   And what makes you think I ever want to see that
           prick again in my life?

RACHEL   You're seeing me.

WILL   Yes but –
           You're…

RACHEL   What?

           Silence.

           They look at each other.

WILL   What are you doing here, Rachel?

RACHEL   I'm looking for Dan.

WILL   But Dan's not here.

RACHEL   No.

WILL   Dan could be anywhere.

RACHEL   Yes.

WILL   I'm the one who's here.

              They look at each other.

              For a long time.

              WILL *reaches over and touches her face.*

              They look at each other.

              She moves away from him.

              She stands up.

              She laughs.

RACHEL   Why do I keep doing this??

WILL   What?

              She looks around the stage.

              She sees DAN.

              She groans.

RACHEL   It would just be nice if it could be my story for
              a change.

WILL   You're telling it aren't you?

RACHEL   Well, I'm trying!
              But look!
              Heroes, everywhere I turn.

WILL   Never said I was a hero.

RACHEL   Yes you did.

WILL   No.

RACHEL   You said you were a superhero.

WILL   I think that might have been you.
              Putting words in my mouth.

RACHEL   You said it!

WILL   According to you.

RACHEL   Are you suggesting I'm an unreliable narrator?

WILL   Well.
              Seems we're getting a slightly biased version
              of events.

RACHEL   Welcome to my world!

WILL   Dan?

              DAN *stands up*.

RACHEL   Excuse me?

WILL   We're here, Dan.

DAN   We're –
              We're here.

RACHEL   Um.
              What are you doing?

WILL   We're here!

              They drink it in.

              They laugh.

RACHEL   Excuse me??

              DAN *and* WILL *embrace*.

              They stare out.

              Hello?

              She doesn't exist.

              She sits down, defeated temporarily.

12

A mountain.

Many years before.

DAN *and* WILL *have reached the top.*

DAN	I can't – It's too – It's too much.
WILL	We did it. We fucking – Fucking did it.
DAN	Is this real?
WILL	I don't fucking know.
DAN	Is this actually FUCKING happening?
WILL	I haven't got a fucking clue.
DAN	It is beyond the realm of fucking reality.
WILL	Jesus fucking Christ.
DAN	Would it be weird if I was sick?
WILL	Do what you fucking want.
DAN	We fucking did it.
WILL	Do you know what this means?
DAN	What does it mean?
WILL	It means… It means…!
DAN	Yes?
WILL	It means we're like fucking invincible!
DAN	Yes!
WILL	We are fucking immortal! We are fucking GODS, Dan!

DAN   YES!

WILL   You and Me, Dan.
           Versus the fucking world.

DAN   Oh my fucking God you're right.

WILL   This, Dan.

           He can't get the words out.

           This.

DAN   I know.

WILL   This is –

DAN   Yeah.

WILL   This is what it's all about.
           All of it.
           Everything.

DAN   I know.

WILL   There isn't anything apart from this.

DAN   Nothing.
           Absolutely nothing.

WILL   We're so fucking lucky.
           To know the truth.

DAN   This is the truth.
           Right here.
           This is the truth.

WILL   Nothing else matters.

DAN   I couldn't give a shit about anything else.

WILL   This is all we need.
           Ever.

DAN   Yes.
           You're right.

           Pause.

           Thank fucking Christ we figured it out.

RACHEL *steps forward.*

She looks at DAN.

WILL *sits down.*

13

DAN *has returned.*

DAN   Sorry.

           Silence.

           I'm really sorry.

RACHEL   Your shoes.

DAN   What?

RACHEL   They're bleeding.

           He looks at his shoes, puzzled.

DAN   I was on the motorway for a bit.
           Then I think I was in…
           Maybe Epping Forest?
           I don't know.

RACHEL   Here.

           She goes to him.

           She starts to take off his shoes.

           He winces.

           She fetches water and a cloth.

           Sit.

DAN   I feel better.
           I just feel so much better.

RACHEL   Sit still.

           She starts to wash the blood off his feet.

DAN   I just really –
           Ow.
           I just really needed that.
           To do that.
           Oh I just feel a million times better!
           You look so beautiful.
           Hello.
           Sorry, did you try and call me?
           My phone was…
           I saw an owl!
           It was stalking its prey and then it –
           Whoosh!
           You weren't worried, were you?
           It was kind of frightening.
           The owl, I mean.
           Cos I was fine.
           This is just what I do.
           I mean, you know that don't you?
           This is just something I need to do and then I'm
           alright again.
           Good as new.

RACHEL   Your toenail's coming off.

DAN   Huh?

RACHEL   Your toenail.

DAN   Oh, yeah!
           That happens all the time.

           She washes his feet.

           That's really nice.

           She stops for a moment.

           Then she carries on.

           You're so lovely.
           I'm tired.
           Do you mind if I close my eyes?

           He closes his eyes.

           I'm just going to close my eyes for a bit.

Slowly RACHEL *continues to wash his feet.*

They are quiet.

She washes his feet.

Silence.

RACHEL   Six days, Dan.

She waits to see if he will say something.

He doesn't.

I hate this role I play.

Silence.

I'm just Penelope.
Aren't I?

She washes his feet.

Knitting my own shroud.
Unpicking it every night.
Waiting for Odysseus.
Waiting for you.

She washes his feet.

One day I might not be.

Silence.

Do you know that?

Pause.

Do you know that, Dan?

DAN*'s eyes are closed.*

She pauses a moment.

She rips off his toenail.

14

The mountain.

The present.

WILL *and* DAN.

WILL *is injured.*

Badly.

WILL   Shall we count how many ways there are to die on the mountain?

             Pause.

             Death by falling.

DAN   Yes.

WILL   Death by freezing.

DAN   Yes.

WILL   Death by starving.
             By slipping.
             By sleeping.

DAN   Yes.

WILL   Don't let me go to sleep.

DAN   I won't.

WILL   Ask me another one.
             Dan.
             Dan?

DAN   Seven times six.

WILL   Is forty-two.

             Pause.

             You can fall down crevasses.
             Get buried in snow.
             In rocks.
             Choke on your own larynx.
             Another one?
             Dan?

DAN   Eight times –
        Eight times twelve.

WILL   Is ninety-six.

DAN   Yes.

WILL   If you make a bad decision.

DAN   Yes.

WILL   I made a bad decision.

DAN   No.

WILL   I can't move it.

DAN   It'll be alright.

WILL   I can't move it, Dan.

DAN   I know.

WILL   I don't know where we are.

DAN   It's –
        Not your fault.

WILL   Yes.
        It is.

        Pause.

DAN   I could go and get –
        Help.

WILL   Where from?

        Silence.

DAN   I could maybe –
        Tie a rope to you and –
        And pull you along.
        Behind me.

WILL   We know how that story ends.

        Silence.

Look at us.

Silence.

Why did we ever think we were a good team?

Pause.

DAN   Because we –
        We were.
        We are.

WILL   Were we ever even friends?

DAN   What sort of a question's that?

WILL   You consider yourself my friend?

DAN   Yes.
        Yes.

        Silence.

WILL   Keep thinking about John Clare.
        The mad poet.
        So mad they locked him up in a lunatic asylum
        in Essex.
        But he escaped.
        Took him four days to get from the asylum back
        home to his village.
        He lived on grass and leaves.
        He'd lie down at night with his head facing north
        so he knew which way to go in the morning.
        He was going home to Mary-Joyce.
        His beloved.
        He kept the picture of his beloved's face in his
        mind's eye and it kept him going.
        He was full of joy.
        But he hadn't seen Mary-Joyce since he was a child.
        Mary-Joyce, in fact, was dead.
        Long dead.
        He had a wife though.
        Her name was Patty.
        But he'd forgotten about her.

At one point, when he was only a few miles from home…
A woman jumped down from a cart and grabbed his arm.
She begged him to come home to her, to their child, but he shook her off.
He didn't know this woman.
He'd never seen her before in his life.
She was ugly, terrible.
She was Patty.
They locked him back in the asylum.
And that's where he died.
Alone.
Homeless.
Without roots.

DAN   I'm sorry.

WILL   For what?

DAN   That I didn't…
        That I…
        Sorry.

        Silence.

WILL   It's alright.

        They wait.

DAN   I want to give her everything.

        Pause

        But I can't.

WILL   No.

DAN   It's like, when I picture a house.
        On a street.
        I picture me outside the house.
        And I'm looking up at an open window.
        And I can hear a baby.
        It's screaming.
        And a woman's voice.
        Pleading with the baby.

I can hear the panic.
In her voice.
And I'm looking up at the window.
My key's in the lock.
And then all of a sudden I'm turning round.
I'm walking.
Back the way I came.
And I get faster and faster and faster.
Until I can't hear it.
The baby, the voice.
I can't hear them and then I can actually breathe again.
The only way to keep breathing is to keep moving.
That's the only thing that's ever worked.

Silence.

WILL   You stupid, selfish man.

DAN   What?

WILL   You blind bloody fool.

DAN stares at him.

Listen to yourself.

DAN   But...

WILL   I don't want to hear it.

DAN   I, I thought you'd understand I –

WILL   I don't.
Want to hear it.

Silence.

WILL *looks at* RACHEL

Why am I only getting my redeeming moment so near the end?

RACHEL *just looks at him.*

What really happened?

RACHEL   When?

WILL   With you and him.

RACHEL   You saw.

WILL   Maybe I need to see it again.

Pause.

Go on.
It's my dying wish.

RACHEL *thinks for a minute.*

She turns to DAN.

RACHEL   Fuck it.
I'll give it all up.
For you.

DAN   Will you?

RACHEL   I already have actually.

DAN   Already?

RACHEL   It's cancelled.

DAN   Really?!

RACHEL   The flight.
The apartment.
The entire Ph.D!
I cancelled it all.

They throw their arms around each other.

DAN   I did too.

RACHEL   You did?!

DAN   I burned the maps.
The plans.
The plane tickets.

RACHEL   You didn't!

DAN   I did!
Just burned them all up!

RACHEL   I burned my notes.

DAN   I slashed my backpack.

RACHEL	I threw my laptop out the window.
DAN	I broke my skis in half and stuffed them in a recycling bin down the street.
RACHEL	I missed a very, very important tutorial –
DAN	Did you?
RACHEL	Cos I was doing fiendish things to you in that bed.
DAN	I didn't meet Will when I was supposed to and I didn't even call.
RACHEL	Ah yes. The drink.
DAN	The 'explain everything, let's be friends' drink.
RACHEL	You had the best intentions.
DAN	He left me all these voicemails.
RACHEL	You didn't even listen to them.
DAN	He got on the plane to Peru by himself and I didn't even care.
RACHEL	They gave my job to someone else, someone I've always hated. And it was like I didn't even notice.
DAN	It doesn't even register.
RACHEL	Because I gave it all up.
DAN	I gave it all up.
RACHEL	It seemed like the only thing at the time.
DAN	Yes…
RACHEL	It made sense…
DAN	We're young, we're in love.
RACHEL	Hey, it happens.
DAN	That's romance for you!
RACHEL	Can't argue with that!

A hesitation.

So…
So now what are we left with?

DAN   I don't know.
             Not much.

RACHEL   Is that good…?

DAN   I've got you.

RACHEL   Yes.

DAN   And you've got me.
             So that's everything really.
             Isn't it?

             They look at each other.

RACHEL   Have you started eating the snow yet?

DAN   What?

RACHEL   If you're really desperate.

DAN   I'm not desperate.
             I'm just waiting.

RACHEL   For what?

DAN   For you.

RACHEL   But I'm not coming.

DAN   Yes you are.
             Look!
             You have!

RACHEL   I'm not doing this any more.

DAN   It's like the story.

RACHEL   Sorry.

DAN   *The Ballad of Tam Lin.*

RACHEL   I hate him.

DAN   What??

RACHEL   I hate Tam Lin.

DAN   No you don't!

RACHEL	He rapes her.
DAN	Because of the curse!
RACHEL	He rapes her.
DAN	Because of the Queen of the Fairies. Janet rescues him from the Queen.
RACHEL	Maybe I never was Janet.
DAN	She holds him fast.
RACHEL	Maybe I'm the Queen.
DAN	No.
RACHEL	Maybe that necklace I gave you is the curse.
DAN	No. The necklace keeps me safe.
RACHEL	You never should have trusted the Queen.
DAN	You don't mean it.
RACHEL	You must beware her smile.
DAN	You don't mean it, you don't, you don't.
RACHEL	He just wants to carry on with his raping and pillaging unrumbled.
DAN	No.
RACHEL	Who did you trample to get up here?
DAN	No one!
RACHEL	You need a lot of money.
DAN	Yes but – It's not like that.
RACHEL	Where did the money come from?
DAN	I – I don't know. Will got it.
RACHEL	Smiling men in pinstripe suits. Handshakes. Luxury flats.

DAN   I don't know!
             There's always money.
             If people want to give it to us then what are we
             meant to do...?

RACHEL   Pull at the string and what do you find?
             What bodies are dangling at the end?

DAN   I don't ask where the money comes from.
             Alright?

RACHEL   As long as you keep conquering it doesn't matter.

DAN   That's not fair.

RACHEL   You can just shut your eyes.

DAN   I didn't.
             I don't.

RACHEL   No wonder you're so miserable.

DAN   I –
             I'm not miserable.

RACHEL   The lines lead back and back and back...

DAN   What do you want me to say?

RACHEL   The same story.
             Again and again.

DAN   I'm sorry.

RACHEL   Hey, I'm no better.
             I fell for it.

             After a while she goes to him.

             She puts her arms around him.

             She leans her head into his chest.

             They sit.

             Sometimes, you see...
             It felt like an invasion.
             Like I was losing whole chunks of land.
             To you.

DAN   I'm sorry.

RACHEL   Like history was swallowing me up.
           First Will's.
           Then yours.
           The the whole world's.

           She reaches over and picks up his pack.

DAN   What are you doing?

           She puts the pack on her back.

           Rachel?
           I need that.

           She holds out her hand.

           He smiles, relieved.

           Goes to take her hand.

RACHEL   No.

DAN   No?

RACHEL   I want the necklace.

DAN   What?

RACHEL   You never wore it anyway.

           He puts his hand over the St Christopher.

DAN   Yes I did.

RACHEL   You took it off.

           Before.

DAN   Yes.
           But that was only because –

RACHEL   Because you thought it claimed you.

DAN   No.

RACHEL   You thought I claimed you.

DAN   I didn't.

RACHEL   Maybe I did.

DAN   I never thought that.

RACHEL   Maybe we both did.
            Maybe that's just what happens.

            She is still holding her hand out.

            Slowly DAN *takes the necklace off and hands it
            to* RACHEL.

            She fastens it around her neck.

DAN   Where are you...
            Where are you going?

            He watches her.

            She turns and looks at him.

            She waits.

            What?

            She turns to WILL.

RACHEL   And you as well.

WILL   Me?

RACHEL   Yes.

            WILL *and* DAN *look at each other.*

            They look confused.

RACHEL   You're not needed any more.

DAN   What?

RACHEL   You can go.

WILL   But that...
            Doesn't make any sense.

            RACHEL *waits.*

            You're not even on this mountain!

RACHEL   Where am I then?

DAN   You're –
            You're at home!

RACHEL   No.

WILL and DAN look at each other.

DAN   Where are we going?

RACHEL   I don't know.
Wherever you like.

DAN   Will you be there?

RACHEL turns away.

Then...
Then what's the point?

RACHEL   Does there always have to be a girl?
Does she always have to be the prize?

Pause.

DAN   It's... it's dangerous out there.

RACHEL   Yeah.

DAN   Will you be careful?

RACHEL doesn't answer.

She hands DAN a piece of paper.

He takes it, puzzled.

RACHEL   Read it.

DAN   What?

RACHEL   Read it.

After a moment, DAN reads from the piece of paper.

DAN   The woman is alone on the ship.
The man is on the shore.
His hand is raised.
She lifts her hand and waves back.
She watches him until he becomes a speck.

DAN hesitates.

He looks at RACHEL.

He looks at WILL.

WILL *and* DAN *exit*.

RACHEL *is alone*.

The End.

A Nick Hern Book

Pilgrims first published in Great Britain in 2016 as a paperback original by Nick Hern Books Limited, The Glasshouse, 49a Goldhawk Road, London W12 8QP, in association with HighTide Festival Theatre, Theatr Clwyd, Vicky Graham Productions and The Yard Theatre

Pilgrims copyright © 2016 Elinor Cook

Elinor Cook has asserted her right to be identified as the author of this work

Cover image by Rebecca Pitt

Designed and typeset by Nick Hern Books, London
Printed in the UK by Mimeo Ltd, Huntingdon, Cambridgeshire PE29 6XX

A CIP catalogue record for this book is available from the British Library

ISBN 978 1 84842 599 6

CAUTION   All rights whatsoever in this play are strictly reserved. Requests to reproduce the text in whole or in part should be addressed to the publisher.

Amateur Performing Rights   Applications for performance, including readings and excerpts, by amateurs in English should be addressed to the Performing Rights Manager, Nick Hern Books, The Glasshouse, 49a Goldhawk Road, London W12 8QP, *tel* +44 (0)20 8749 4953, *email* rights@nickhernbooks.co.uk, except as follows:

Australia: Dominie Drama, 8 Cross Street, Brookvale 2100, *tel* (2) 9938 8686, *fax* (2) 9938 8695, *email* drama@dominie.com.au

New Zealand: Play Bureau, PO Box 9013, St Clair, Dunedin 9047, *tel* (3) 455 9959, *email* info@playbureau.com

South Africa: DALRO (pty) Ltd, PO Box 31627, 2017 Braamfontein, *tel* (11) 712 8000, *fax* (11) 403 9094, *email* theatricals@dalro.co.za

United States of America and Canada: The Agency (London) Ltd, see details below

Professional Performing Rights   Applications for performance by professionals in any medium and in any language throughout the world (and amateur and stock performances in the United States of America and Canada) should be addressed to The Agency (London) Ltd, 24 Pottery Lane, Holland Park, London W11 4LZ, *fax* +44 (0)20 7727 9037, *email* info@theagency.co.uk

No performance of any kind may be given unless a licence has been obtained. Applications should be made before rehearsals begin. Publication of this play does not necessarily indicate its availability for amateur performance.